# In True Crypto Fashion

Chelsea Von Schneden

Copyright © 2022 by Chelsea Von Schneden

**All rights reserved.**

No part of this publication may be reproduced, stored or transmitted in any form or by any means, electronic, mechanical, photocopying, recording, scanning, or otherwise without written permission from the publisher. It is illegal to copy this book, post it to a website, or distribute it by any other means without permission.

# Contents

Introduction ................................................. 7

**Chapter 1: Dressing Up Your Knowledge Wardrobe** .................................................. 11

    Understanding Blockchain: The Foundation Garment of Crypto............................................. 12
    Distributed Network: The Fabric of Trust......... 12
    Encryption: The Zipper That Protects Your Data .................................................................... 13
    Consensus Mechanisms: The Dress Code Everyone Agrees On............................................. 13

**Chapter 2: Bitcoin vs Ethereum - The Denim Jeans and Classic Blazer of Crypto** ................... 15

    Bitcoin: The Classic Denim Jeans ..................... 15
    Ethereum: The Versatile Blazer ........................ 16
    Tokens vs Coins: Statement Pieces vs Basics ... 17

**Chapter 3: Choosing Your Style: Tailoring Your Investment Portfolio to Fit Your Financial Runway** ......................................................... 19

    Conservative Classics: Blue-Chip Cryptocurrencies................................................. 20

Bitcoin (BTC): The Original Trailblazer aka The Classic Denim Jeans of Crypto – ...................... 20
Ethereum (ETH): The Smart Contract Pioneer aka The Versatile Blazer That Complements Any Outfit - ................................................................ 21
Diversifying Your Crypto Wardrobe ................ 21
Trendy Picks: Altcoins ...................................... 22
Litecoin (LTC), Cardano (ADA), Polkadot (DOT): The Seasonal Must-Haves! ................... 23
High Fashion Risk-Takers: ICOs & DeFi Projects ............................................................................. 24
Embracing Trends While Managing Risks ....... 24

## Chapter 4: Fashioning Your Financial Safe: Picking the Perfect Crypto Wallet for Your Valuables ................................................................. 26

Types of Crypto Wallets: From Casual Clutches to Secure Safes ................................................. 26
Choosing Your Perfect Fit When selecting a crypto wallet: ...................................................... 32
Fashionable Tips For Setting Up Your Crypto Wardrobe Accessory ......................................... 32

## Chapter 5: Accessorizing Your Portfolio: Selecting Your First Crypto Gem ........................... 34

## Chapter 6: The Fabric of Community ................. 37

Cryptocurrency Communities: The Designers, Tailors, and Trendsetters Developers: .............. 37
Stitching Your Place Within Crypto Couture ... 38

**Chapter 7: Dress Code Regulations – Legal and Ethical Considerations in Crypto** .......................... 40

    The Fashionable Compliance ........................... 40
    Ethical Sourcing: A Lesson from Fashion......... 41
    Navigating Legal Waters.................................... 41
    The Role of Self-Regulation.............................. 42
    The Global Runway of Compliance .................. 42

**Chapter 8: Making Crypto Your Own – Embracing Personal Style in the Digital Realm ..44**

**About The Author** .................................................. 47

# Introduction

The Runway Debut: Discovering Cryptocurrency

In a world where the traditional tapestry of finance is being rewoven, there emerges a vogue so bold and avant-garde that it has piqued the imagination of investors and innovators alike. It is Cryptocurrency—a domain where flair meets function, and style intertwines with substance. Welcome to "In True Crypto Fashion," where we dress to impress upon the blockchain. Just as haute couture marks its presence on the runway with a blend of artistry and audacity, cryptocurrencies debuted with similar panache.

Bitcoin strutted down the financial runway in 2009, turning heads with its revolutionary design—a peer-to-peer electronic cash system that promised freedom from the constraints of traditional banking practices. This was not just a new look; it was an entirely new way to think about money. Daring, digital, decentralized—crypto set the stage for an entire industry of altcoins to follow suit. Currently this market is dominated by men, It is my mission to change that.

In the world of cryptocurrency, women have historically been underrepresented. However, recent statistics show a growing trend towards greater female participation in this emerging market. According to various studies, women currently make up around 20% of cryptocurrency users and investors. While this number is encouraging, there is still much progress to be made in achieving gender equality within the industry. There are several compelling reasons for women to gain knowledge about the crypto industry to create a more inclusive environment where all voices are heard and valued.

Firstly, by understanding cryptocurrencies and blockchain technology, women can actively participate in shaping the future of finance and technology. By acquiring knowledge and skills in this field, they can contribute their unique perspectives and ideas to drive innovation. Secondly, gaining expertise in crypto empowers women financially. Cryptocurrencies offer new opportunities for investment and wealth creation that were previously inaccessible or limited for many individuals. By being knowledgeable about this market, women can take control of their financial futures and build wealth on their own terms.

Furthermore, as more industries embrace blockchain technology and cryptocurrencies become increasingly integrated into our daily lives, it becomes essential for everyone to have a solid understanding of these concepts. This knowledge will enable people to navigate the changing landscape effectively and make informed decisions regarding digital assets. Lastly, but most importantly, promoting diversity within the crypto industry is crucial for its long-term success. Including more women brings diverse perspectives that foster creativity and innovation while challenging existing norms.

I believe a primary reason why women are underrepresented in this market is due to....time. Women are just as capable of understanding blockchain concepts as men, but we generally have less expendable time. To be a conscientious investor, it is important to read and research the market. Because crypto is such a new and unknown concept, I found it challenging to find reputable research materials in the first place. Because I could not find content, I realized there was a need for a guidebook. Personally, I comprehend and respond best to a new concept when it is presented in familiar analogies. If you have similar proclivities, and fashion is your language of choice, I am here to use those concepts to teach you the fundamentals of crypto quickly and effectively.

My intention is to provide this brief handbook for starting your crypto journey. An easy to read and understand how-to guide that will not feel like a chore. My hope is that you can juggle multiple real-life responsibilities and will finish it. I hope you will use this as your crypto compact to reapply your knowledge foundation whenever needed.

## Chapter 1

# Dressing Up Your Knowledge Wardrobe

Before any important fashion event, we meticulously comb through our closets, inspecting each garment and contemplating the perfect ensemble. Similarly, in the crypto industry, we meticulously research and analyze various cryptocurrencies, examining their features and potential, to curate the ideal investment portfolio.

Understanding the Basics: Just as you wouldn't wear socks with sandals (unless that's your statement!), don't dive into crypto without understanding the basics. What is blockchain? How does Bitcoin differ from Ethereum? We'll lay down these fashion fundamentals so you can strut confidently into crypto conversations.

## Understanding Blockchain: The Foundation Garment of Crypto

Blockchain technology is indeed the foundation garment of the cryptocurrency world. Much like a well-crafted white T-shirt is essential to a versatile and functional wardrobe, it's simple yet sophisticated, unassuming yet powerful. To truly appreciate its role in the digital currency ecosystem, let's delve deeper into these key elements and understand how they interweave to create a robust and reliable system.

## Distributed Network: The Fabric of Trust

The distributed nature of blockchain is like a fabric woven from multiple threads – each thread represents a computer or node within the network. Just as no single thread can make up the entire fabric, no single node controls the blockchain. This creates redundancy; if one node fails or acts maliciously, others maintain integrity. Imagine attending an event where everyone knows each part of your outfit – from your white T-shirt to your statement shoes. If someone claimed you were wearing red instead of white, others would immediately refute it because they all have seen it for themselves. Similarly, in blockchain technology, every participant has access to the entire transaction history ensuring transparency and collective verification.

**Encryption: The Zipper That Protects Your Data**

Encryption in blockchain is like that trusty zipper on your favorite pair of jeans – it secures what needs to be kept safe while allowing easy access when necessary. When information is added to a blockchain, it's encrypted into complex codes through cryptographic hash functions. These functions transform data into unique strings of characters that are nearly impossible to reverse-engineer without authorization—much like trying to guess exactly how many stitches are in your T-shirt without unraveling it completely! This level of security ensures that once transactions are recorded on the blockchain they remain confidential and immutable.

**Consensus Mechanisms: The Dress Code Everyone Agrees On**

In any social setting there's often an unspoken dress code—a consensus about what's appropriate attire for different occasions whether casual or formal wear. Blockchain uses consensus mechanisms as its own 'dress code' for validating transactions before adding them onto the ledger. One popular mechanism is Proof-of-Work (PoW) used by Bitcoin which involves solving complex mathematical puzzles— think about buttoning up all buttons correctly under time pressure! Another method Proof-of-Stake (PoS) requires users (stakeholders) who hold more currency—or have more 'skin in the game'—to validate transactions similar perhaps to giving those with VIP passes at fashion shows more say over trends! Each mechanism has its pros and cons, but their purpose remains consistent—to reach agreement across all nodes about which transactions are legitimate ensuring only stylishly 'appropriate' ones make their way onto our metaphorical runway—the ledger itself!

Understanding these foundational aspects helps demystify how blockchains operate beneath their surface complexity much like knowing what goes into making that perfect white T-shirt gives us appreciation beyond just its look or feel against our skin! With this knowledge we can confidently navigate conversations around crypto understanding why this technology holds such transformative potential not just for finance but numerous other industries too—it's truly haute couture within digital innovation.

Chapter 2

# Bitcoin vs Ethereum - The Denim Jeans and Classic Blazer of Crypto

In the fashion-forward world of cryptocurrency, Bitcoin and Ethereum stand out as the quintessential wardrobe essentials comparable to denim jeans and a classic blazer. Each has its unique style, purpose, and versatility that cater to different needs within the crypto closet.

**Bitcoin: The Classic Denim Jeans**

Introduced to the world in 2009 by an enigmatic creator known only as Satoshi Nakamoto, Bitcoin emerged as the original piece in every crypto enthusiast's collection. Much like a pair of well-fitted denim jeans, it is lauded for its simplicity and durability. It was crafted with one primary function in mind—to serve as digital gold; a store of value that could be exchanged directly between peers without any need for traditional financial intermediaries such as banks or governments. Bitcoin's blockchain is like the sturdy fabric from which these jeans are cut—resilient against wear-and-tear (fraudulent transactions) due to its robust decentralized network and secure cryptographic practices. It's designed to be universally wearable (accepted), transcending borders just like a timeless pair of Levi's transcends fleeting fashion trends.

**Ethereum: The Versatile Blazer**

If Bitcoin is your reliable pair of jeans, then Ethereum would undoubtedly be your stylish blazer—introduced later but bringing additional functionality and flair into your wardrobe. Conceived by Vitalik Buterin with its launch in 2015, Ethereum extended beyond simply recording transactions on its ledger; it introduced smart contracts into the mix. Imagine smart contracts as those custom patches or embellishments you add onto your blazer —they not only enhance its aesthetic but also expand what you can do with it. These self-executing agreements have terms embedded within their code that automatically enforce themselves once predetermined conditions are met—no middle man required. This innovation opened up possibilities for decentralized applications (dApps) on Ethereum's platform much like how accessorizing can transform an outfit from daywear to evening chic. With this added layer comes greater complexity but also more opportunities for creativity within the ecosystem.

**Tokens vs Coins: Statement Pieces vs Basics**

Venturing deeper into our sartorial analogy:

Coins, including Bitcoin itself or Ether (the native currency on Ethereum), are akin to those fundamental pieces we reach for day after day—the white T-shirt under our leather jacket or our trusty blue jeans.

Tokens, on the other hand, represent assets built upon existing blockchain platforms such as ERC-20 tokens created on top of Ethereum's infrastructure. They're comparable to statement accessories—a bold watch or an eye-catching belt—that serve specific functions or make particular statements about their wearer's style preferences.

As we dress ourselves in this digital attire:

1. We must guard our private keys with utmost care—they're equivalent to securing the combination lock on our wardrobe where all valuables lie.
2. We should remain aware that market volatility mirrors fashion trends—what may be en vogue today could very well fall out-of-style tomorrow.

3. We must always conduct diligent research before investing—as one would scrutinize material quality or read garment reviews prior making an online purchase decision.

By grasping these fundamentals—the white T-shirt (blockchain), denim jeans (Bitcoin), leather jacket (Ethereum), versatile accessories (smart contracts), statement pieces versus basics (tokens vs coins)—you'll be well-dressed for any crypto conversation!

CHAPTER 3

# CHOOSING YOUR STYLE: TAILORING YOUR INVESTMENT PORTFOLIO TO FIT YOUR FINANCIAL RUNWAY

Are you more conservative or a risk-taker in style and investments? We'll explore different cryptocurrencies and investment strategies to find what suits your personal flair best. Just as in fashion, where your personal style might range from conservative classics to avant-garde, your approach to investing in cryptocurrencies can vary based on your risk tolerance and preferences. Let's explore how different cryptocurrencies and investment strategies align with various fashion styles.

## Conservative Classics: Blue-Chip Cryptocurrencies

When it comes to investing in cryptocurrencies, there's a certain allure to the tried and true—the "blue-chip" cryptos. These are the digital assets that have proven their worth over time, much like those classic pieces in your wardrobe that never go out of style. Let's delve into these conservative classics and understand why they might be a good fit for your financial portfolio.

## Bitcoin (BTC): The Original Trailblazer aka The Classic Denim Jeans of Crypto –

Established Legacy: Just as a pair of comfortable jeans is a must-have in any wardrobe, Bitcoin is the original cryptocurrency that started it all. It has established itself as the leader of the pack.

Widespread Acceptance: Across the globe, Bitcoin is recognized and accepted by individuals and businesses alike; similar to how a white shirt fits seamlessly into various social settings. –

Resilience Over Time: Despite market fluctuations, Bitcoin has shown remarkable resilience, akin to how a quality pair of jeans withstands wear and tear.

**Ethereum (ETH): The Smart Contract Pioneer aka The Versatile Blazer That Complements Any Outfit -**

Smart Contracts: Ethereum introduced smart contracts to the world—a game-changer for blockchain applications just like how adding a blazer can transform an outfit.

Foundation for Innovation: Many new projects are built on Ethereum's platform. It's become foundational in crypto fashion much like how blazers are essential in traditional fashion.

Adaptability & Growth Potential: With ongoing updates aimed at improving scalability and efficiency (like Ethereum 2.0), this crypto shows promise for growth similar to how styles evolve with trends while maintaining their core essence.

**Diversifying Your Crypto Wardrobe**

While blue-chip cryptocurrencies offer stability relative to their more speculative counterparts, diversification remains key:

1. Mix High-Quality Pieces with Trendy Items: Just as you'd pair timeless clothing with seasonal accessories for balance, consider mixing blue-chips with select altcoins or tokens from emerging sectors.

2. Understand What You Own: Know your investments inside out—just as you would check care labels on clothes before laundering them—to avoid unpleasant surprises down the line.
3. Balance Risk Wisely: Have reliable staples but don't shy away from occasionally trying something new; just ensure it doesn't dominate your closet—or portfolio.
4. Think Long-Term Fashion vs Fast Fashion: Some pieces last years; others fade quickly after several uses. Similarly assess whether each crypto investment has long-term potential or if it's likely just a short-term trend. Investing in conservative classics within cryptocurrency means opting for assets that have stood up against challenges over time—much like those indispensable items we reach for time and again when dressing up our personal style!

**Trendy Picks: Altcoins**

For the fashion-forward and trendsetters, altcoins are the crypto runway's latest designs. These alternative coins to Bitcoin and Ethereum are like the fast-fashion trends that pop up each season—bold, new, and full of potential. They capture attention with their unique features and promise of quick returns but beware—their allure may fade as quickly as last season's fads.

## Litecoin (LTC), Cardano (ADA), Polkadot (DOT): The Seasonal Must-Haves!

## The Statement Pieces of Your Crypto Collection

- Litecoin (LTC): Think of this as a pair of knock off sneakers that suddenly everyone must have, but not everyone can afford. Litecoin offers faster transaction times compared to Bitcoin, making it a popular choice for those looking for both style and practicality.
- Cardano (ADA): Consider this eco-friendly fashion—innovative and conscious about its impact. With a focus on sustainability, scalability, and transparency, Cardano aims to be the blockchain that thinks about tomorrow.
- Polkadot (DOT): Polkadot can be seen as a fashion event or platform that fosters collaboration and connectivity among diverse blockchains, just as a fashion event brings together designers and enthusiasts in the real world. It allows different blockchains to interact, creating an ecosystem where ideas and innovation can flourish, much like fashion collaborations push the boundaries of creativity.

**High Fashion Risk-Takers: ICOs & DeFi Projects**

For those who dare to wear haute couture or bespoke tailoring:

ICOs: Investing in an ICO can feel like you're getting an exclusive preview at a high-end designer's showroom before their collection hits mainstream boutiques. The potential for reward is significant if you discover the next big name in fashion—or crypto—but so is the risk if they don't become popular with the public.

DeFi Projects: These are your custom-made garments crafted from experimental fabrics; they're innovative financial services built on blockchain technology without banks or brokers in between—revolutionizing finance just as avant-garde designs revolutionize fashion.

**Embracing Trends While Managing Risks**

When adding these trendy altcoins or cutting-edge projects into your investment mix:

1. Stay Informed About The Latest: Keep up-to-date with market news just like you would follow fashion blogs or magazines—to spot what's hot.
2. Know When To Let Go: Just like last season's trends might not work this year, be prepared to

move on from investments that no longer show promise.
3. Balance Your Portfolio: Mix these exciting picks with more stable investments—the equivalent of pairing bold accessories with classic outfits—to maintain a well-rounded portfolio.
4. Understand The Unique Qualities: Each altcoin has its own "style" based on its technology and use case; appreciate what makes each one special before adding it to your collection.

Altcoins offer investors an opportunity to spice up their portfolios with some flair—analogous to how one might incorporate statement pieces into their wardrobe for added zest! However, always remember that while trends can make for exciting times—and potentially profitable ones—they also come with risks that should be carefully considered within one's overall investment strategy.

# Chapter 4

# Fashioning Your Financial Safe: Picking the Perfect Crypto Wallet for Your Valuables

Just as you wouldn't leave the house without a purse or wallet to keep your cash and cards safe, entering the world of cryptocurrency requires a secure place to store your digital assets. Picking out your first crypto wallet is like choosing the perfect accessory—it needs to be functional, suit your style, and match your security needs. You may use one or more of these at the same time.

**Types of Crypto Wallets: From Casual Clutches to Secure Safes**

**Hot Wallets (Online Wallets):**

The Chic Clutch

Hot wallets are the chic clutches of the cryptocurrency world—sleek, connected, and perfect for those who need their digital assets at their fingertips for swift transactions. These are often mobile wallets on your smartphone or web-based wallets through cryptocurrency exchanges. Let's take a stroll through the boutique of hot wallets available on various platforms:

**1. Mobile Wallets:**

- Coinbase Wallet: This is your versatile crossbody bag that not only stores a diverse array of cryptocurrencies but also lets you mingle with decentralized applications (dApps) in style.
- Trust Wallet: The signature wallet from the house of Binance, Trust Wallet is like an all-access pass to crypto's latest trends, supporting a multitude of currencies and featuring a built-in Web3 browser to explore dApps.
- Exodus: A multi-currency wallet that prides itself on its aesthetic appeal as much as its functionality—think of it as your go-to designer wallet that works seamlessly across mobile and desktop.

**2. Web Wallets:**

- Blockchain.info: A vintage piece in the web wallet collection, Blockchain.info offers classic support for Bitcoin, Ethereum, and other staples in your crypto wardrobe.
- MyEtherWallet (MEW): Like having a custom-made outfit from an open-source atelier, MEW allows you to tailor your interactions with the Ethereum blockchain directly via your web browser.
- MetaMask: Primarily catering to Ethereum enthusiasts, MetaMask serves as both a sophisticated purse for your coins and an exclusive pass into the world of dApps through its elegant browser extension.

### 3. Desktop Wallets:

- Electrum: Known for being lightweight yet durable—It can be likened to a lightweight, durable, and timeless fashion accessory that prioritizes efficiency, security, versatility, and user-friendliness. Its simplicity, reliability, and continuous development make it a popular choice among crypto enthusiasts for securely managing their digital assets.
- Atomic Wallet: Imagine this as your extensive jewelry box—with support for

over 300 cryptocurrencies and offering atomic swaps—a true treasure chest for those who value variety.

### 4. Exchange Wallets:

- Binance: Upon joining the Binance platform runway show, you're gifted with an on-trend hot wallet where you can showcase various cryptocurrencies featured by this leading exchange brand.
- Kraken: Much like Binance's offering but with Kraken's unique flair—this exchange provides patrons with their very own hot wallet upon joining their elite club. While hot wallets provide convenience akin to slipping into loafers instead of lacing up boots—they do come with caution tags; they're generally less secure than cold storage options because they're more exposed to potential cyber pickpockets such as hackers or phishing scams.

To keep these fashionable accessories secure:

- Fasten them tightly with strong passwords
- Add layers like two-factor authentication (2FA)
- Regularly update them just like refreshing one's seasonal wardrobe
- For high-value collections or long-term investments consider transitioning some pieces

into cold storage options such as hardware or paper wallets—the equivalent of moving valuables from daily wear drawers into safety deposit boxes at banks!

**Pros**: Hot wallets are like tote bags—accessible, convenient, and perfect for everyday use. They're connected to the internet, making transactions quick and easy.

**Cons**: However, just as a tote bag can be vulnerable to pickpockets in a crowded space, hot wallets can be susceptible to online threats such as hacking.

### Cold Wallets: The Couture Vaults of Crypto

Imagine cold wallets as the haute couture of crypto storage—exquisite, handcrafted pieces that are less about everyday wear and more about preserving your most valuable digital assets with the utmost elegance and security.

Examples:

- Ledger Nano X: Consider this hardware wallet as the equivalent of a bespoke, armored evening clutch. It's sleek, portable, and designed with state-of-the-art security features to protect a wealth of cryptocurrencies on the go.
- Trezor Model T: This is like an exclusive safety deposit box in a high-fashion

accessory form. With its intuitive touchscreen interface and robust security protocols, it's crafted for those who seek luxury in both design and peace of mind.
- KeepKey: Picture KeepKey as your timeless piece from an artisan jeweler—robust yet refined. It offers a simple interface encased in a polished metal body, turning heads while keeping your digital treasures locked away.

**Pros**: Cold wallets are the silk-lined jewelry boxes of the crypto universe, offering a luxurious and secure enclave for your digital treasures.

**Cons**: Much like an exquisite but heavy ball gown, cold wallets provide superior protection at the expense of day-to-day convenience and accessibility.

Each cold wallet is similar to an investment piece from the runway shows—a blend of artistry and assurance that provides unrivaled protection for your cryptocurrency collection. In summing up this chapter on cold wallets, think of them as the ultimate fashion statement in crypto security—a perfect blend of style and substance. While they come with their own set of considerations such as accessibility and usability, these devices offer unparalleled protection that mirrors the exclusivity and luxury one finds in high-fashion pieces. For those who view their digital currency investments as a collection worth showcasing only in the finest settings, cold wallets provide just the right combination of flair and fortress-like security.

**Choosing Your Perfect Fit When selecting a crypto wallet:**

1. Consider Your Activity Level: Are you trading daily (needing an easily accessible tote) or storing value long-term (requiring a safe box)?
2. Assess Security Needs: How much value will you store? More valuable collections require stronger protection.
3. Think About Convenience: Will you need quick access on-the-go? If so, mobile options might suit you best.
4. Plan For Backups: Like having an extra pair of shoes in case one breaks a heel unexpectedly—you should have backup options ready.

**Fashionable Tips For Setting Up Your Crypto Wardrobe Accessory**

- Choose something that complements your style—a user-friendly interface, if simplicity is key, or advanced features, if complexity doesn't faze you.
- Secure it well! Use strong passwords and enable two-factor authentication—like adding both a lock and an alarm system to safeguard against intruders.

- Keep software updated—stay current with trends not only in fashion but also in technology updates which patch up vulnerabilities just like mending tears before they become bigger problems!
- Write down recovery phrases—Recovery Phrases are a group of secret words that the exchange, wallet or company provides you with to reset your account or password if lost. This is the only way to recover an account without a password. These should be kept in a safe or in multiple safe locations should you need them. They are the equivalent of keeping spare buttons; these phrases help restore access if something goes wrong with the original "accessory."

In conclusion: Your first crypto wallet choice sets the tone for how securely and conveniently you'll interact with digital currencies—it's essential not only from a practical standpoint but also reflects personal preferences much like fashion does! Whether opting for hot wallets' ease-of-use or cold ones' robust security measures—or perhaps somewhere in between—it's about finding what fits best within one's lifestyle while ensuring peace of mind knowing that investments are well-dressed by adequate protection measures!

## Chapter 5

# Accessorizing Your Portfolio: Selecting Your First Crypto Gem

Just as a discerning fashion enthusiast would carefully choose the perfect accessory to complement their ensemble, selecting your first cryptocurrency requires a blend of taste, research, and attention to detail. Here are the steps you should elegantly glide through before adding that sparkling crypto gem to your financial wardrobe:

1. Understand Your Style: Before diving into the crypto bazaar, define what you're looking for in an investment. Are you drawn to the timeless elegance of Bitcoin, much like a classic little black dress? Or do you prefer the bold statement of an altcoin that could be likened to avant-garde haute couture?

2. Educate Yourself on Trends: Stay abreast of market trends and educate yourself on blockchain technology—understanding these can be as crucial as knowing the difference between prêt-à-porter and custom tailoring.
3. Assess Risk Tolerance: Just like choosing between a daring heel or a comfortable flat, assess your risk tolerance. Cryptocurrencies can be volatile; ensure that your choice aligns with how much uncertainty you're willing to walk with.
4. Set Your Budget: Decide on your budget beforehand—much like setting aside funds for an exclusive runway piece—to avoid getting swept away in the moment and spending more than intended.
5. Choose Reputable Platforms: Opt for well-established exchanges with robust security measures—a bit like shopping at high-end boutiques where authenticity is guaranteed over back-alley deals where it's not.
6. Diversify Thoughtfully: Consider starting small or diversifying across different 'styles' of cryptocurrencies; after all, even in fashion, it's wise not to put all your eggs in one basket—or all your jewels in one box.
7. Stay Informed on Regulations: Keep up-to-date with regulations regarding cryptocurrency

investments in your region—similar to knowing import taxes and duties when ordering international fashion items online.

When ready to make that first purchase, here are some U.S.-based exchanges—think of them as esteemed boutiques—where you can shop for your crypto gem:

- Coinbase: Much like walking into a flagship store on Fifth Avenue; it offers ease-of-use for beginners.
- Binance.US: This is akin to visiting an upscale department store—it has extensive offerings catering to various tastes.
- Kraken: With its robust security features and deep liquidity pools, Kraken is comparable to an exclusive jeweler known for exquisite pieces.
- Gemini: Think of Gemini as that boutique which prides itself on user experience and elegant design—a place where newcomers feel welcomed.

As you select from these reputable venues and take those initial steps towards purchasing cryptocurrency, remember: acquiring digital assets is about creating a portfolio that reflects both current trends and personal conviction—the same way curating a wardrobe blends seasonal must-haves with timeless classics.

## Chapter 6

# The Fabric of Community

Now that you've adorned your portfolio with its first shimmering crypto asset, it's time to weave yourself into the vibrant tapestry of the community. Just as fashion is not merely about garments but also about the culture and connections they inspire, cryptocurrency thrives on communal exchange for insights, trading tips, and emerging projects. The Runway of Collaboration In both realms—crypto and couture—community involvement is paramount. It's where patterns are shared, trends are set, and voices merge to create a collective narrative. Engaging with these communities can enrich your understanding and appreciation for the nuanced artistry behind each 'piece'.

**Cryptocurrency Communities: The Designers, Tailors, and Trendsetters Developers:**

These are the master tailors of code in the crypto world; they stitch together blockchain protocols like artisans crafting bespoke suits. Their forums are akin to ateliers where knowledge is honed and innovations take shape.

Traders: Much like fashion buyers who anticipate what will next dominate boutiques' racks, traders analyze patterns to predict which cryptocurrencies will rise in value. They often gather in online marketplaces or discussion boards—the stock exchanges of digital currency—to exchange strategies.

Artists (NFT Creators): In this digital renaissance, artists mint NFTs as one-of-a-kind pieces that capture imagination much like avant-garde runway shows. They form collectives reminiscent of exclusive gallery openings where enthusiasts can appreciate new expressions of creativity.

Enthusiasts & Advocates: These individuals are comparable to lifestyle influencers in fashion—they share their passion through blogs or social media channels and often guide newcomers through their journey into this chic financial sphere.

**Stitching Your Place Within Crypto Couture**

To truly invest in cryptocurrency beyond mere acquisition means intertwining yourself within its community fabric:

1. Join forums or social media groups focused on cryptocurrency discussions.

2. Attend virtual meetups or webinars hosted by thought leaders.
3. Follow developers' updates on platforms such as GitHub.
4. Explore trading platforms with integrated community features for live chats.
5. Visit online galleries showcasing NFTs to support digital artists.
6. Participate in blockchain events or conferences when possible.

By engaging with these diverse threads within the crypto ecosystem—just as one would immerse themselves into fashion week parties or designer workshops—you'll gain a deeper understanding not only of your investments but also become part of shaping what comes next on this dynamic runway. Remember that every interaction weaves you further into this intricate network—a place where each member contributes to a larger pattern that defines both current movements and future legacies within cryptocurrency's stylish revolution.

# Chapter 7

# Dress Code Regulations – Legal and Ethical Considerations in Crypto

Having familiarized yourself with the fundamentals, safeguarded your crypto assets using a new wallet, and acquired your first valuable digital currency, it is now imperative to understand and abide by the rules governing the world of cryptocurrency. Just as fashion has its dress codes and ethical considerations, the world of cryptocurrency also has its own set of regulations and ethical guidelines that must be followed.

**The Fashionable Compliance**

In the world of fashion, certain events or venues may have specific dress codes—black-tie affairs demand formal attire while casual gatherings allow for more relaxed outfits. Similarly, in the world of cryptocurrency, compliance with legal regulations is essential. Understanding the regulatory landscape surrounding cryptocurrencies is crucial to ensure you are operating within legal boundaries. Governments around the world are continuously developing frameworks to address issues such as taxation, money laundering prevention, investor protection, and consumer rights.

## Ethical Sourcing: A Lesson from Fashion

Fashion enthusiasts have become increasingly conscious about where their garments come from—demanding transparency about labor conditions and sustainability practices. In crypto terms, this translates into considering ethical sourcing of tokens. Just as you would research a clothing brand's supply chain to ensure fair labor practices or environmentally-friendly materials were used, it's important to evaluate cryptocurrencies based on their underlying technology and principles. Look for projects that prioritize decentralization, privacy rights protection, or contribute positively toward social impact initiatives.

## Navigating Legal Waters

Just as designers must navigate intellectual property laws when creating new collections or trademarks for their brands, participants in the crypto space must navigate legal waters surrounding intellectual property rights related to blockchain technology patents or copyright infringement concerns tied to NFTs (non-fungible tokens).

Additionally, tax regulations vary across jurisdictions when it comes to buying/selling cryptocurrencies or earning income through mining activities. Understanding tax obligations ensures compliance while avoiding any potential penalties.

**The Role of Self-Regulation**

Fashion industry bodies often establish self-regulatory measures like sustainable fashion certifications or ethical sourcing guidelines. Similarly, the crypto community has taken steps towards self-regulation through initiatives like industry standards for security practices or codes of conduct for exchanges and projects. Participating in these self-regulatory efforts can help foster a more trustworthy and responsible crypto ecosystem, much like adhering to fashion industry standards promotes sustainability and fair practices.

**The Global Runway of Compliance**

Just as fashion trends transcend borders, compliance with legal and ethical considerations in crypto is a global affair. As you navigate the world of cryptocurrency, it's important to stay informed about regulatory developments in different countries. Engaging with local communities, attending conferences or webinars on regulatory updates can provide valuable insights into compliance requirements specific to your region. By staying ahead of the curve, you can ensure that your crypto journey remains both fashionable and compliant.

As we conclude this chapter on dress code regulations—legal and ethical considerations in the world of cryptocurrency—remember that just as fashion evolves over time, so do regulations surrounding digital assets. Stay informed, adapt to changes gracefully, and continue embracing this exciting intersection between technology and finance while upholding integrity along the way.

## Chapter 8

# Making Crypto Your Own – Embracing Personal Style in the Digital Realm

In this final chapter, we have explored the exciting concept of making crypto your own by infusing personal style into your journey in the digital realm. We have delved into the parallels between fashion and cryptocurrency, discovering how both offer opportunities for self-expression, creativity, and growth. Throughout this book, we have learned about the basics of cryptocurrency, securing our assets with wallets, making strategic investments, understanding blockchain technology, and navigating the ever-changing landscape of this digital revolution. But it is in this chapter that we truly understand how to make our mark on this world by embracing personal style.

Just as fashion allows us to curate our wardrobes to reflect our unique tastes and personalities, so too can we curate our crypto portfolios to align with our values and interests. By carefully selecting cryptocurrencies that resonate with us on a deeper level—whether it be environmentally conscious projects or decentralized finance—we create a crypto identity that is uniquely ours. We have explored how mixing trends in both fashion and cryptocurrency can lead to exciting possibilities. Just as blending different styles creates an eclectic ensemble in fashion, diversifying our portfolio with established cryptocurrencies alongside promising altcoins can create a well-rounded investment strategy tailored to our goals.

Accessories play an essential role in completing any fashionable look. In the same vein, non-fungible tokens (NFTs) serve as accessories for your digital wallet—adding personality and uniqueness to your crypto journey. We discovered how NFTs allow us to collect pieces that resonate with us or even create our own NFTs as a form of self-expression. Building connections has always been crucial in both fashion and cryptocurrency. Just as networking opens doors for collaborations within the fashion industry, engaging with like-minded individuals through online communities or attending blockchain conferences allows us to gain insights while forging meaningful relationships within the crypto space. As we conclude this book, we understand that just as fashion is ever-evolving, so too is the world of cryptocurrency. We must remain adaptable and open-minded, embracing new technologies and staying informed about emerging projects. By doing so, we can continue to evolve our crypto style and make a lasting impact in this dynamic landscape.

Remember, your journey in the digital realm is not just about following trends but also setting them. Embrace your unique ideas and perspectives, contribute to the community's growth, and become an influential voice within the crypto space. Your personal touch and belief in the transformative power of blockchain technology will shape the future of cryptocurrency. As a takeaway, I encourage you to embrace your crypto style with confidence and authenticity. Just as fashion allows us to express our individuality, cryptocurrency offers a platform for self-expression within a technological landscape. Craft your own crypto identity, curate your portfolio with care, and let your choices reflect who you are and what you believe in. Remember that crypto, just like fashion, is not just about the clothes we wear or the projects we invest in—it's about how they make us feel.

# About The Author

Chelsea Von Schneden is a wife, mother of two, entrepreneur and a passionate advocate for women in the world of cryptocurrency. In 2021 she took a leap into the world of crypto and has never looked back. Her journey into the male-dominated financial sector of cryptocurrency ignited a fire within her to bring more women into this exciting and extremely profitable space.

As an entrepreneur and business owner, Chelsea understands the importance of financial empowerment and believes that cryptocurrency has the potential to level the playing field for individuals from all walks of life. She is dedicated to making investing in crypto simple to understand and more accessible for those who may feel intimidated or excluded due to their gender or financial means.

Chelsea's own success as an investor and trader in the crypto market has inspired her to share her knowledge and experience with others. Through her series of books, she aims to empower women by providing them with the tools and inspiration they need to learn about the crypto market, make informed investment decisions and build generational wealth.

With a genuine passion for education and advocacy, Chelsea strives to break the barriers in the crypto space. She believes that diversity is essential for innovation and growth within any industry. By encouraging more women to participate in cryptocurrency investing , she hopes to create a more inclusive environment within the space where everyone can thrive.

Chelsea's mission is clear, she wants every woman who desires financial independence through investing not only to have access, but to also feel confident navigating this exciting digital landscape.

Through her own journey as a wife, mother and business owner, Chelsea embodies resilience and determination. She understands firsthand how important it is for women not only to invest, but to take control over their financial futures.

Chelsea hopes to serve as an inspiration and role model to other women that they too can succeed in this rapidly evolving world of cryptocurrency.

www.ingramcontent.com/pod-product-compliance
Lightning Source LLC
Chambersburg PA
CBHW050027230526
45470CB00003B/1161